W9-BPN-291

Sep 20

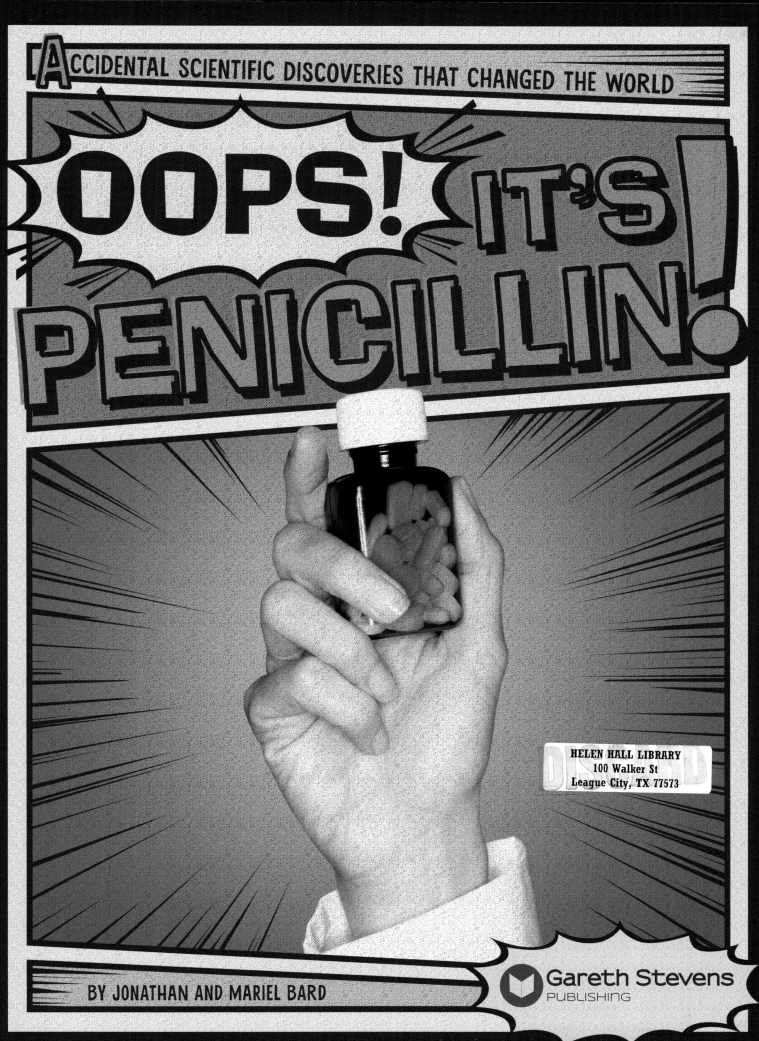

Please visit our website, www.garethstevens.com. For a free color catalog of all our high-quality books, call toll free 1-800-542-2595 or fax 1-877-542-2596.

Library of Congress Cataloging-in-Publication Data

Names: Bard, Jonathan, author. | Bard, Mariel, author.
Title: Oops! it's penicillin! / Jonathan and Mariel Bard.
Other titles: Oops! it is penicillin!
Description: New York : Gareth Stevens, [2020] | Series: Accidental
   scientific discoveries that changed the world | Includes bibliographical
   references and index.
Identifiers: LCCN 2018047092| ISBN 9781538239902 (pbk.) | ISBN 9781538239926
   (library bound) | ISBN 9781538239919 (6 pack)
Subjects: LCSH: Fleming, Alexander, 1881-1955–Juvenile literature. |
   Penicillin–Juvenile literature. | Antibiotics–Juvenile literature. |
   Discoveries in science–Juvenile literature.
Classification: LCC RS165.P38 B37 2020 | DDC 615.3/295654–dc23
LC record available at https://lccn.loc.gov/2018047092

First Edition

Published in 2020 by
Gareth Stevens Publishing
111 East 14th Street, Suite 349
New York, NY 10003

Designer: Katelyn E. Reynolds
Editor: Monika Davies

Photo credits: Cover, p. 1 IAN HOOTON/Science Photo Library/Getty Images; cover, pp. 1–32 (burst) jirawat phueksriphan/Shutterstock.com; cover, pp. 1–32 (burst lines) KID_A/Shutterstock.com; p. 5 Daily Herald Archive/SSPL/Getty Images; p. 7 JRJfin/Shutterstock.com; p. 9 Kateryna Kon/Shutterstock.com; p. 13 Britannica Kids (http://kids.britannica.com/elementary/art-87568/Louis-Pasteur-performs-a-scientific-experiment)/Tungsten/Wikipedia.org; pp. 15 (both), 21 (main) Bettmann/Getty Images; p. 17 sirtravelalot/Shutterstock.com; p. 19 Daily Herald Archive/SSPL/Getty Images; p. 21 (inset) Jacques Boyer/Roger Viollet/Getty Images; p. 23 Science Museum, London (https://wellcomecollection.org/works/apnj2urs?query=penicillin); p. 27 Monkey Business Images/Shutterstock.com; p. 29 Chris Ware/Getty Images.

Printed in the United States of America

CPSIA compliance information: Batch #CS19GS: For further information contact Gareth Stevens, New York, New York at 1-800-542-2595.

CONTENTS

Words in the glossary appear in **bold** type the first time they are used in the text.

ACCIDENTAL BREAKTHROUGHS

What do microwaves, superglue, and chewing gum have in common? They were all accidental discoveries! These items were made possible because something surprising happened.

In September 1928, one very important accidental discovery happened when Dr. Alexander Fleming discovered penicillin. Penicillin is a medicine, or a drug taken to make a sick person well. This medicine is a type of antibiotic, or a drug that can kill germs, including harmful **bacteria**.

Penicillin is the first antibiotic doctors ever used on human patients. Penicillin keeps bad bacteria from growing. Without penicillin, sicknesses caused by bad bacteria would spread. Penicillin has helped save millions of lives around the world. And, it was discovered accidentally!

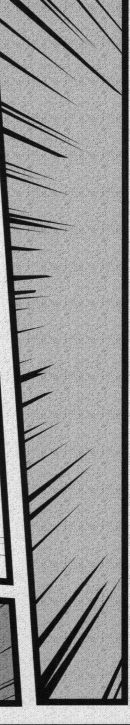

Animal Testing

THE FIRST TESTS OF PENICILLIN AS A MEDICINE WERE DONE ON MICE. THE MICE THAT WERE TREATED WERE CURED OF THEIR SICKNESSES CAUSED BY BAD BACTERIA. MICE AND RATS ARE OFTEN USED AS THE FIRST TEST SUBJECTS FOR NEW TREATMENTS. THIS IS PARTLY BECAUSE THEY ARE SMALL AND CAN QUICKLY GET USED TO A NEW ENVIRONMENT.

You can take penicillin a few different ways, including as a shot, a chewable pill, or liquid you can swallow.

A HIDDEN WORLD

There are millions of tiny **organisms**, called microbes, everywhere around you. You can't see these microbes with your eyes. They are too tiny to be seen! To observe these microbes, you need a microscope, or a tool used to view very small objects so they can be seen much larger and more clearly.

Humans didn't know about microbes for thousands of years. It wasn't until 1665 that English scientist Robert Hooke described a microorganism he saw using an early microscope. Then, in 1676, Dutch scientist Antonie van Leeuwenhoek built a stronger microscope and discovered that microbes are everywhere!

Ancient Cures

BEFORE MODERN ANTIBIOTICS, PEOPLE NEEDED DIFFERENT WAYS TO TREAT INFECTIONS, OR SICKNESSES CAUSED BY GERMS. AT ONE TIME, PEOPLE USED MOLDY BREAD TO TREAT DISEASES, OR ILLNESSES, IN SERBIA, CHINA, GREECE, AND EGYPT. PEOPLE KNEW THIS TREATMENT WORKED, BUT THE EXACT SCIENCE AS TO WHY IT WORKED WOULDN'T BE KNOWN FOR THOUSANDS OF YEARS.

Moldy bread was able to treat infections and diseases because the type of mold that grew was penicillium. This is what penicillin is made from!

GOOD AND BAD MICROBES

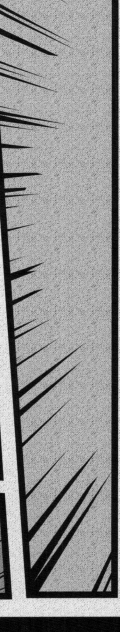

Right now, there are millions of microbes living on and inside your body. Most of these microorganisms are good for us. They help our bodies work properly and can protect us from bad bacteria.

But, these microorganisms can't keep us safe from all bad bacteria. Sometimes, we catch not-so-helpful microorganisms, such as viruses, that cause illness when they enter the body. Bad bacteria cause all sorts of problems. Certain bacterial infections can even be deadly. For thousands of years, there was no way to fight this bad bacteria. These microbes were a major problem for humans—until the discovery of antibiotics.

THE HUMAN MICROBIOME

ALL THE MICROBES THAT LIVE IN AND ON OUR BODIES MAKE UP WHAT IS CALLED THE HUMAN MICROBIOME. THIS INCLUDES MANY TYPES OF MICROBES, SUCH AS THE BACTERIA IN OUR GUT THAT HELPS US BREAK DOWN FOOD. SCIENTISTS ARE STILL STUDYING THE MICROBES OF OUR BODIES TO BETTER UNDERSTAND HOW WE BENEFIT FROM THEM.

There are many types of bad bacteria that can make us sick. For example, the bacteria *Streptococcus pneumoniae* can cause infections in our ears, lungs, sinuses, and blood.

HOW ANTIBIOTICS WORK

Doctors use many different antibiotics, all of which have the same purpose: to weaken or kill bad microbes. Some antibiotics, including penicillin, affect the microbe's cell wall. A cell wall is like skin, meaning it keeps what's inside safe from what's outside. This type of antibiotic weakens the cell walls, causing the microbes to burst and die soon after.

Other antibiotics interrupt a bad microbe's normal activity. For example, some antibiotics focus their attack on certain bacterial **enzymes**, which are needed for the bacteria cells to work correctly. Bad bacteria will try to create new copies of itself, so it can keep spreading through the body. Antibiotics stop this from happening.

THE CELL WALL

MANY ANTIBIOTICS FOCUS THEIR ATTACK ON THE CELL WALLS OF BAD MICROBES. ONLY CERTAIN TYPES OF ORGANISMS HAVE A CELL WALL. THIS IMPORTANT PART OF THE CELL OFFERS STRUCTURE AND PROTECTION FOR THE MICROBE. BUT, IT ALSO ALLOWS CERTAIN THINGS TO PASS THROUGH, SUCH AS **NUTRIENTS**.

ANTIBIOTICS VS. CELL WALLS

This bacterium is growing. Tiny holes sometimes form in the bacterium's cell wall, but the cell is able to repair itself.

Some antibiotics, like penicillin, focus their attack on the bacterium's cell wall. The antibiotic stops the small holes from being fixed.

As more holes go unrepaired, the cell wall gets weaker and weaker.

Soon, water will rush inside the cell, causing it to burst. This kills the bacterium.

11

EARLY PIONEERS OF ANTIBIOTICS

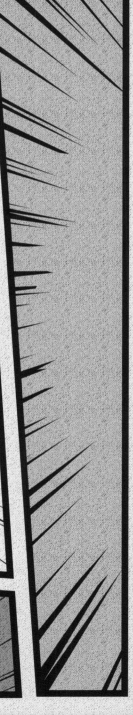

In the late 1800s and early 1900s, researchers realized that bad microbes cause diseases. Many set out to find ways to kill these microbes.

In Germany in the late 1800s, researchers Rudolf Emmerich and Oscar Löw developed an antibiotic and called it pyocyanase. Though it showed promise of working against some diseases, it turned out to be toxic, or poisonous to humans. In 1909, after 606 tests, Paul Ehrlich and his team developed a medicine they named Salvarsan. This treatment was effective as an antibiotic, but it was also toxic.

So, the search for antibiotics continued. This brings us to a messy lab in Scotland, where Alexander Fleming was about to make a very interesting discovery.

Germ Theory

BEFORE WE UNDERSTOOD MICROBES, SCIENTISTS DIDN'T KNOW WHAT CAUSED MOST DISEASES. IN THE 1800S, THE WORK OF LOUIS PASTEUR AND ROBERT KOCH LED TO GERM **THEORY**, WHICH EXPLAINED THAT BAD MICROBES ENTER THE BODY AND CAUSE DISEASE. KOCH ALSO PROVED THAT ONE TYPE OF GERM CAN CAUSE A SPECIFIC DISEASE.

Louis Pasteur was a chemist and **microbiologist**. The process of pasteurization, or heating liquids to kill any bacteria, is named after him!

13

GROSS! MOLD IN THE PETRI DISH

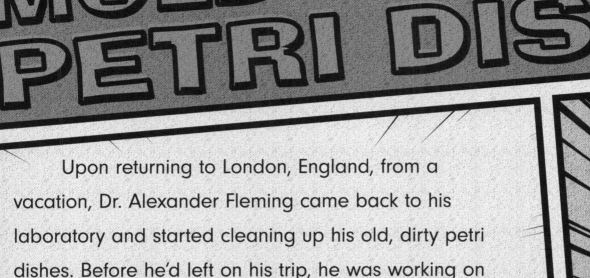

Upon returning to London, England, from a vacation, Dr. Alexander Fleming came back to his laboratory and started cleaning up his old, dirty petri dishes. Before he'd left on his trip, he was working on growing a bacterium called staphylococcus. This is a nasty bacterium that causes people to become very sick.

When Fleming looked down at his petri dishes, he noticed something odd. There was mold growing in one of them! But Fleming noticed that where the mold was growing, staphylococcus was not. He wondered if he might be on to an important discovery. Fleming then tried to repeat the accidental experiment to see if it would happen again.

STAPHYLOCOCCUS

STAPHYLOCOCCUS IS A GROUP OF BACTERIA THAT CAN CAUSE SEVERE HEALTH PROBLEMS. THIS TYPE OF BACTERIA IS ROUND IN SHAPE AND IT LOOKS LIKE GRAPES UNDER A MICROSCOPE. STAPHYLOCOCCUS CAN BE FOUND ON THE HUMAN BODY AND IN MOST PEOPLE'S NOSES. WHEN STAPHYLOCOCCUS CAUSES SOMEONE TO GET SICK, DOCTORS CALL IT A STAPH INFECTION.

A petri dish is a small, circular container with a flat cover. It is often used for growing bacteria. On September 28, 1928, Fleming found this dirty petri dish with penicillium mold. The mold grew on one side of the dish, and the bacteria near the mold died.

15

FLEMING'S FOLLOW-UP EXPERIMENTS

Fleming followed up on his experiments and soon realized that the mold itself wasn't killing the bacteria. However, the mold was producing a "juice." This mold juice, which he would later call penicillin, was responsible for killing off the bacteria. To confirm this, he ran many more experiments with different types of bacteria. Every bacteria he tested died because of the special mold juice.

Fleming spent the next 10 years working on his discovery. But he ran into a big problem. He couldn't create enough of this juice to make a medicine people could use. He had an amazing discovery, but no way to use it!

Mold Juice

Fleming's so-called mold juice is created through a process called secretion. Secretion is when a cell makes a certain kind of matter and then releases it. On a larger scale, crying and sweating are both forms of secretion in humans! In Fleming's case, the mold secreted penicillin, which is what kills bad bacteria cells.

During Fleming's lifetime, even a small scratch could become infected and lead to death. This pushed scientists to work on antibiotics that could attack bacteria that caused infections.

WORKING OUT THE KINKS

After Fleming singled out the mold juice as the key to killing bacteria, he tried to remove everything but pure penicillin from his samples. This proved to be very difficult, and he wasn't successful. Despite this, he announced his discovery of penicillin in a medical journal. However, not many people paid attention.

Then, in 1940, two scientists named Howard Florey and Ernst Chain picked up where Fleming left off. Their first task was **purifying** penicillin. Purifying separates harmful substances from a mixture, leaving only the helpful matter. In this case, it took many gallons of mold "soup" to get just a little bit of pure penicillin.

THE NOBEL PRIZE

FLEMING, FLOREY, AND CHAIN RECEIVED THE 1945 NOBEL PRIZE IN PHYSIOLOGY OR MEDICINE FOR THEIR WORK ON PENICILLIN AS A MEDICINE TO FIGHT INFECTIONS. THE NOBEL PRIZE IS ONE OF THE HIGHEST HONORS A SCIENTIST CAN RECEIVE. THIS TYPE OF NOBEL PRIZE IS AWARDED FOR MAJOR DISCOVERIES THAT OFFER GREAT BENEFITS TO HUMANS.

Florey, Chain, and their team tried to grow penicillin in many different containers, including baths and food tins. These are culture flasks used to grow penicillin in 1943.

19

BREAKTHROUGH: SUCCESS IN PATIENTS!

In their experiments, Florey and Chain showed that penicillin was safe to use in mice, and it could also cure the mice of infections. The real test, though, was to see if penicillin would be safe and effective medicine for humans.

In 1941, Albert Alexander was the first patient given penicillin as a treatment. He was scratched by a thorn while gardening. He developed a bad infection and received some penicillin. Within a day, his infection started clearing up! But penicillin was still very hard to make. Sadly, the hospital ran out of penicillin to treat Alexander's infection, and his infection came back.

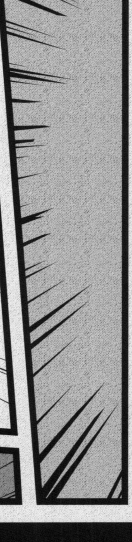

Human Volunteers

NEW TREATMENTS ARE FIRST TESTED ON LAB MICE. BUT TO SEE IF A NEW TREATMENT COULD WORK IN HUMANS, PEOPLE NEED TO VOLUNTEER TO TAKE THE MEDICINE. THE FIRST PATIENT TO TEST PENICILLIN WAS A WOMAN VERY ILL WITH CANCER. PENICILLIN DIDN'T CURE HER DISEASE. BUT DOCTORS LEARNED THAT PENICILLIN IS SAFE FOR HUMANS.

Howard Florey put together a team of six women to help grow penicillin. The "Penicillin Girls" farmed penicillin from hundreds of containers in which mold was growing.

HOWARD FLOREY

PENICILLIN USE DURING WORLD WAR II

During this time, World War II had begun and was in full force. Most of Britain was busy with the war effort. Florey and his team couldn't get much help with their research. In June 1941, he and Norman Heatley traveled to the United States, where Florey had a friend at Yale University named John Fulton.

Fulton connected Florey with the US Department of Agriculture. The department had many large vessels that Florey could use to grow lots of penicillium mold. The US government quickly realized the usefulness of penicillin to the **Allied powers**. The need for antibiotics on the battlefield brought together **laboratories** around the United States, which led to major improvements.

GAME CHANGER

BEFORE ANTIBIOTICS, ONE OF THE BIGGEST KILLERS DURING A WAR WAS INFECTIONS! PENICILLIN GREATLY INCREASED THE SURVIVAL RATE IN HOSPITALS. FOR EXAMPLE, IN WORLD WAR I, 18 PERCENT OF DEATHS WERE FROM BACTERIAL **PNEUMONIA**. THANKS TO PENICILLIN, THAT NUMBER DROPPED TO LESS THAN 1 PERCENT IN WORLD WAR II.

Thanks to PENICILLIN
...He Will Come Home!

This advertisement from World War II appeared in *Life* magazine. It told Americans about the production of penicillin and how it would help the fighting soldiers.

When the thunderous battles of this war have subsided to pages of silent print in a history book, the greatest news event of World War II may well be the discover

THE GOLDEN AGE OF ANTIBIOTICS

Newspapers began calling penicillin a "miracle drug" because of all the lives it saved. Scientists kept searching for and developing other antibiotics to fight infections. During the next several decades, scientists around the world found many more antibiotics that successfully healed patients' infections.

At the same time, antibiotics became widely used in farming. To keep livestock from getting sick, animals on farms in the United States are given around 80 percent of all antibiotics sold.

Nowadays, hundreds of millions of **prescriptions** for antibiotics are given every year. However, we're now realizing that using all of these wonder drugs comes at a cost.

Unneeded Prescriptions

AROUND ONE-THIRD OF THE ANTIBIOTICS PRESCRIBED TO PATIENTS IN DOCTOR'S OFFICES, EMERGENCY DEPARTMENTS, AND CLINICS IN THE UNITED STATES ARE NOT ACTUALLY NEEDED. THIS EQUALS ABOUT 47 MILLION UNNECESSARY PRESCRIPTIONS! MOST OF THESE ARE CASES OF COLDS, SORE THROATS, AND SOME SINUS AND EAR INFECTIONS. THESE CASES ARE CAUSED BY VIRUSES—NOT BACTERIA. ANTIBIOTICS WON'T HELP!

THE RISE OF ANTIBIOTICS

Pre-1800 — ANCIENT CULTURES USE MOLDY BREAD TO TREAT INFECTIONS.

1800s — LOUIS PASTEUR AND ROBERT KOCH DEVELOP GERM THEORY.

1909 — PAUL EHRLICH DEVELOPS SALVARSAN, BUT IT'S TOO TOXIC TO USE IN HUMANS.

1928 — FLEMING ACCIDENTALLY DISCOVERS PENICILLIN BECAUSE OF MOLD GROWING IN A PETRI DISH.

1940 — HOWARD FLOREY AND ERNST CHAIN READ FLEMING'S WORK. WITH THE HELP OF THEIR TEAM, THEY PURIFY PENICILLIN.

1941 — ALBERT ALEXANDER IS THE FIRST PATIENT TO RECEIVE PENICILLIN AS A TREATMENT.

FLOREY AND NORMAN HEATLEY TRAVEL TO AMERICA FOR HELP IN PRODUCING LARGE AMOUNTS OF PENICILLIN.

1942 — ANNE SHEAFE MILLER IS THE FIRST AMERICAN PATIENT TO USE PENICILLIN AND IS CURED OF HER INFECTION.

1940s — PENICILLIN PRODUCTION TAKES OFF, SAVING MILLIONS OF LIVES DURING WORLD WAR II.

1950s–1970s — NEW ANTIBIOTICS ARE DISCOVERED AND PRESCRIBED TO PATIENTS.

2000s–Present — GROWING CONCERNS REGARDING ANTIBIOTIC OVERUSE AND **RESISTANCE** LEAD TO FEWER ANTIBIOTICS PRESCRIBED.

ANTIBIOTIC RESISTANCE

Antibiotics are very helpful to sick patients all around the world. However, there is one huge problem: the more we use antibiotics, the stronger bacteria can become! This is called antibiotic resistance. Bacteria are just like any other living organism. They want to survive. Bacteria develop resistance, a natural process where bacteria learn how to fight against new dangers—including antibiotics.

Bacteria can become resistant to antibiotics when antibiotics are used too much or incorrectly. For example, your doctor might give you enough antibiotics for 10 days. But if you use only 2 days' worth, the antibiotics may only kill the weaker bacteria. This leaves stronger bacteria behind.

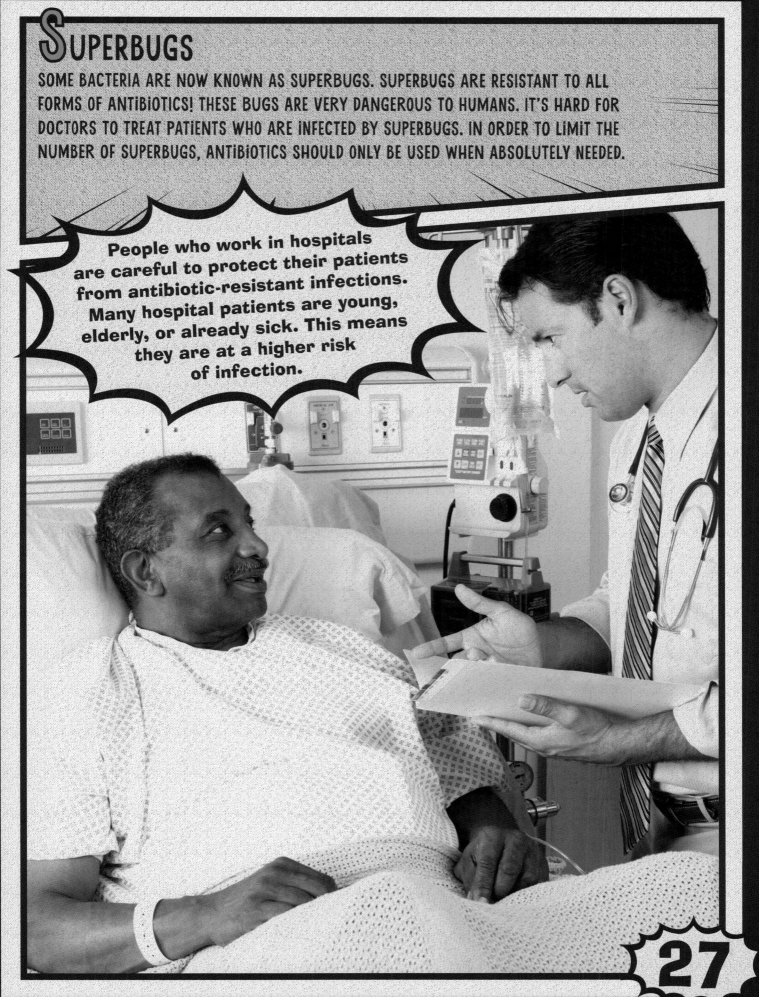

SUPERBUGS

SOME BACTERIA ARE NOW KNOWN AS SUPERBUGS. SUPERBUGS ARE RESISTANT TO ALL FORMS OF ANTIBIOTICS! THESE BUGS ARE VERY DANGEROUS TO HUMANS. IT'S HARD FOR DOCTORS TO TREAT PATIENTS WHO ARE INFECTED BY SUPERBUGS. IN ORDER TO LIMIT THE NUMBER OF SUPERBUGS, ANTIBIOTICS SHOULD ONLY BE USED WHEN ABSOLUTELY NEEDED.

People who work in hospitals are careful to protect their patients from antibiotic-resistant infections. Many hospital patients are young, elderly, or already sick. This means they are at a higher risk of infection.

THE POWER OF MOLD JUICE

Maybe you've scraped your knee and then applied antibiotic cream to your skin. Or, you might have gotten an ear infection and had to take antibiotics. Think about how that medicine may have saved your life!

Penicillin started as an accidental discovery in a messy lab. This discovery turned into one of the biggest breakthroughs in medical care the world has ever seen. Small cuts no longer turned into big infections. There was a cure for infectious diseases. All of this was thanks to some mold growing in a petri dish—and the efforts of many scientists who believed in the power of mold juice!

Mold Isn't Always Bad

LIFESAVING MEDICINE COULD BE ROLLING AROUND IN YOUR REFRIGERATOR RIGHT NOW! IT MIGHT LOOK LIKE BLUE, FUZZY MOLD GROWING ON A CANTALOUPE. OF COURSE, YOU SHOULDN'T EAT MOLDY BREAD, LEMONS, OR CANTALOUPE. HOWEVER, YOU CAN TRY BLUE CHEESE. THIS TYPE OF CHEESE IS MADE WITH PENICILLIUM MOLD AND IS SAFE TO EAT.

Although Fleming is known best for his discovery of penicillin, he was also an artist. Instead of using paint, he used different-colored bacteria!

GLOSSARY

Allied powers: the group of nations, including England and the United States, in World War II that opposed the Axis nations, including Germany and Japan

bacteria: tiny creatures that can be seen only with a microscope

enzyme: matter made in the body that helps certain actions necessary for life to occur

laboratory: a place with tools to perform experiments

microbiologist: a scientist who studies tiny organisms, such as bacteria

nutrient: something a living thing needs to grow and stay healthy

organism: a living thing made up of one or more cells

pneumonia: a serious illness that affects the lungs and makes it hard to breathe

prescription: a written message from a doctor that tells someone to use a specific medicine or remedy

purify: to make something pure by removing harmful chemicals

resistance: the opposition or prevention of something

sinuses: any of several spaces in the skull mostly connected with the nostrils

theory: an idea suggested or presented as possibly true but that is not known or proven to be true

For More Information

BOOKS

Biskup, Agnieszka. *Medical Marvels: The Next 100 Years of Medicine*. North Mankato, MN: Capstone Press, 2017.

Eamer, Claire. *Inside Your Insides*. Toronto, ON: Kids Can Press, 2016.

Mould, Steve. *The Bacteria Book*. London, UK: DK Children, 2018.

WEBSITES

Penicillin: Who Found This Functional Fungus
www.kidsdiscover.com/quick-reads/penicillin-found-functional-fungus
Learn more about Alexander Fleming's accidental discovery of penicillin and the antibiotic's beginnings as "mold juice."

What Are Antibiotics?
mocomi.com/how-do-antibiotics-work
Discover interesting facts about antibiotics and how they work.

What Are Germs?
kidshealth.org/en/kids/germs.html
Find out about the different types of germs, including bacteria, viruses, fungi, and protozoa!

Index